BEN DORAIN

a conversation with a mountain

About the Author

Garry MacKenzie is a poet and non-fiction writer based in Fife, Scotland. His poetry has been published in journals and anthologies including *Antlers of Water, The Clearing, The Compass Magazine* and *Dark Mountain*. He was awarded an Emerging Scottish Writer Residency at Cove Park in 2019, and is a recipient of a Scottish Book Trust New Writers Award. He has won the Robert McLellan Poetry Competition and the Wigtown Poetry Competition, and his book *Scotland: a Literary Guide for Travellers* is published by I.B. Tauris. He has a PhD in contemporary landscape poetry, and teaches creative writing and literature.

BEN DORAIN

a conversation with a mountain

GARRY MACKENZIE

With introductions by Kathleen Jamie and Meg Bateman,
and the Gaelic of Duncan Bàn MacIntyre

THE IRISH PAGES PRESS
CLÓ AN MHÍL BHUÍ
2021

Ben Dorain:
a conversation with a mountain
is first published in hardback
on 18 January 2021.

The Irish Pages Press
129 Ormeau Road
Belfast BT7 1SH
Ireland

www.irishpages.org

Editors: Chris Agee, Meg Bateman and Kathleen Jamie

Typeset in 12/15 pt Monotype Perpetua.
Designed and composed by RV, Belfast. Printed by Bell & Bain, Glasgow.

A CIP catalogue record for this book
is available from The British Library.

Dust-jacket images: "Ben Dorain" by Seán Purser
and author photography courtesy of Garry MacKenzie

ISBN: 978-0-9935532-8-8

In memory of Marco Dees (1984-2018)

While now we talk as once we talked
   Of men and minds, the dust of change,
   The days that grow to something strange,
In walking as of old we walked

Beside the river's wooded reach,
   The fortress, and the mountain ridge,
   The cataract flashing from the bridge,
The breaker breaking on the beach.

Tennyson, *In Memoriam A.H.H.*

CONTENTS

I

II

I

FOREWORD

Garry MacKenzie

I have lived with Duncan Bàn MacIntyre's poem *Moladh Beinn Dòbhrain* for several years. I first encountered it through anthologised excerpts of Iain Crichton's Smith's 1969 translation, with its haiku-like, imagistic stanzas and its embrace of a rhyme scheme reminiscent of MacIntyre's Gaelic. In 2014 I was commissioned to write a literary travel guide to Scotland and, having acquired sufficient Gaelic to read the original poem with the help of Dwelly's Gaelic-English dictionary, included my own translation of its opening lines in that book. I had initially been attracted by the poem's rootedness in a West Highland landscape which I knew well, and also by its metrical intricacy and rhetorical grandeur. I wanted to provide non-Gaelic readers with an English-language representation of MacIntyre's skill as a poet.

The longer I spent with *Moladh Beinn Dòbhrain*, however, the more the poet's craftmanship became subordinate to his intense focus on the natural world. There's no ego in this poem: instead, a Highland mountain and its herd of red deer are observed with what might be called an early kind of environmental awareness. Its eight sections describe the mountain, the seasons, and the life cycle of the herd. There is detailed information about diet, such as the freshest streams to drink from and the deer's preference for plants including St John's wort and tormentil. The animals are presented as individuals, with differing appearances, personalities and eccentricities. They can be heard barking, bellowing and calling to their young. They rut, play, and flee from the hunt. Throughout the poem the natural world is evoked in a way which is unsentimental and literal. Deer are deer, rocks are rocks, and there is little symbolism or metaphor. In its commitment to close observation, *Moladh Beinn Dòbhrain* sits comfortably alongside biologist Frank Fraser Darling's landmark field study *A Herd of Red Deer* (1937). That old trope of mountain poetry, the enraptured bard on the peak, surveying the landscape below, is entirely absent. The summit of Ben Dorain isn't even mentioned.

After publishing my travel book, complete with twelve lines translated from *Moladh Beinn Dòbhrain*, I felt I had unfinished business with the poem. Several fine translations, including those by Crichton Smith, Hugh MacDiarmid and Alan Riach, have sought to emphasise the musicality and formal complexity of MacIntyre's achievement. But I wanted to do something new, and produce a translation which centred on its relatively unmediated evocation of the phenomenal world. It's a poem of light and life and movement, teeming with biodiversity but nevertheless conscious of the ways in which humans interact with their environment, for good and for ill. Rather than create an English equivalent of MacIntyre's poetic form, which is modelled on the repetitions and embellishments of pibroch music, I wanted to explore how a completely new, open form might draw out the ecological content of the original and position it in a modern poetic context.

In the resulting work, *Ben Dorain: a conversation with a mountain*, my free translation of MacIntyre's verse, based on the Gaelic text of Angus Macleod's *Orain Dhonnchaidh Bhain* (1978), is on the left hand side of each page. On the right is new material which responds to, challenges or elaborates upon the translation. These right-hand sections incorporate the language of contemporary environmental philosophy and ecological science, details relating to modern Highland land use, deer mythology from several cultures, and references to the Gaelic tradition of nature poetry. To take an anachronistic liberty (and my *Ben Dorain* takes a few), if MacIntyre's *Moladh Beinn Dòbhrain* can be compared to rap lyrics due to its repetitions, obsessive rhyme scheme and rhythmical intensity, then my ecological version of it is more like acid jazz or the hip-hop music underlying rap: a process that samples, alters, embellishes and hybridises a recognisable original. My version of *Ben Dorain* is intended as a respectful conversation between a 250-year-old poem and the modern world, in which various voices and traditions speak alongside each other and to each other.

Autumn 2020, Crail, Fife

INTRODUCTION
Kathleen Jamie

Ben Dorain: a conversation with a mountain is the first full-length work published by Scottish poet Garry MacKenzie. It appears in this handsome edition courtesy of The Irish Pages Press, which is a new presence in Scottish poetry publishing. The press is associated with the journal *Irish Pages* which for two decades has been an important and intelligent contributor to the cultural life of these islands.

When we say "these islands", we think we know what we mean, but *Irish Pages*, as journal, press and arts festival, is alert to an alternative map reading. It seeks to link what Editor Chris Agee calls the "dissident peripheries". Moving between the Republic of Ireland, Northern Ireland and Scotland, the journal is also concerned with wider Europe, the Balkans in particular, and North America. It considers ancient nations and languages, emerging ecologies and reconsidered identities.

We are alive at a time of sudden, necessary reappraisals, and changes of direction. History is far from over, the future struggles to find its shape. Change is happening, whether it be local, in the fracturing of the United Kingdom, or across the wide sweep of history, as revealed by the truths and hopes of the Black Lives Matter movement. It is happening on a planetary level, in the perils of climate change and species loss. Have human beings ever known such a moment?

When we may feel as though our species and our planet are cascading into a future unknown, and uncertainty is all about, it may seem odd to publish a book which is "a conversation" with a mountain, the very symbol of solidity. The mountain is Ben Dorain, which rises near Bridge of Orchy. It appears as a Fuji-esque cone from some angles. The conversation is also with a praise poem composed 250 years ago, by Duncan Bàn MacIntyre. MacIntyre's poem is a musical paean to this one particular Scottish mountain and its deer. The original poem is in Gaelic, a language no longer spoken on that mountainside. (There, in that one fact, you have your political and power shifts, your economic and cultural push and shove.) But what Garry MacKenzie has done, in this wonderful book, is to revivify that poem. He has created a new "inhabited music" which springs MacIntyre's work into the present day. It's not a translation, nor a modernised version, though there is that also. He has opened MacIntyre's mountain poem like a geode, to use a geological term, and he has created an environmentally-aware, science-informed poetic counterpoint in English, which he presents dancing along with MacIntyre's re-expressed eighteenth-century vision. Like the deer they so admire, the two poets' lines leap back and forth across the page, across times, across languages, across species and poetic forms. It is a new work which alerts us to the tradition, which is to say, to the consciousness of the past. It calls this consciousness into the present, so that its wisdom might strengthen us for the environmental challenges to come.

Who knows what future? Our times would have been unimaginable to Duncan Bàn MacIntyre. When he composed his poem, we were already on the way to species loss, to environmental degradation. His Ben Dorain deer may have known Scotland's last wolves, which are variously said to have been extirpated in the seventeenth century, or the eighteenth or maybe even the nineteenth. (MacIntyre was himself a gamekeeper.) But who knows if they might not one day be returned? Who would have thought, 50 years ago, that huge tracts of Scottish land, mountain ranges and moorland, their populations cleared, land held in a few private (wealthy) hands, might be taken into community ownership, and managed for nature? Who knows what the "dissident peripheries" will think of next?

But this is not primarily a political work. This is a work of love: of landscape and animals and poetry. Despite the shifting grounds which surround it, Ben Dorain the mountain remains true and centred, its marvellous creatures marvellously observed.

Autumn 2020, Newburgh, Fife

BEN DORAIN

a conversation with a mountain

If you are going to observe an animal you must know it well.
  — Frank Fraser Darling, *A Herd of Red Deer*

It is never we who affirm or deny something of a thing; it is
the thing itself that affirms or denies something of itself in us.
  — Spinoza, *Short Treatise II*

In the art of the great music, the drone is eternity, the tune
tradition, the performance the life of the individual.
  — Thomas A. Clark, "Riasg Buidhe"

PART ONE: GROUND

How does it begin?
With the piper's drone
with the coarse fabric of the land
  in greens and greys and purples,
the lines of hoof and song
   that cross it.

Landscape as pibroch:
the drone never silent,

     never still,

then fingered notes
soar up over the moor:

Of all the high places
    I praise Ben Dorain,
in beauty she towers above other bens.

I can't get enough of her –

    look with me

at the graceful sweep of land where the deer hold court,
at the woods, those grassy groves where they browse

      (kingdom of cuckoo, wren and chaffinch)

at the mountain's gleaming face.

Look at the white-rumped team, with the hunt in pursuit –
they catch news on the wind and are gone.

Over there is a stag who knows his mind,
a deep one   who doesn't need to brag.

He cuts a fine figure,
at home in his own skin,
that summer coat of rich unfading red
like a royal seal.

This is the ground,
the theme of the hill's
great music,
                  laid down
in layers like lacquer,
like myth, like the work
of a wasp on its paper nest.

If the hill could listen to itself
would it hear at the pace
that lichen grows?
                  Would it be tuned
to the slow dark mouths of moss on stone?

Here is Ben Dorain:
        deer in their generations come and go
        with their rituals of sedge
        and dwarf-willow; wolves are here
        and in the downhill inch
        of a boulder they're gone;
        volcanoes echo   and now there's man

This is what you need to kill a stag:
a rifle that's in working order
a marksman in his prime, someone who knows
        how to pull a trigger.

The gun should have a good notched flint
screwed firm into the hammer;
      a cock that strikes true
against the frizzen plate;
an eight-sided barrel you can trust;
a gunstock of unblemished walnut
      that fits snug against the shoulder.

This way you'll fell the most agile stag
– but you need a real craftsman, a specialist in deer;
one who'll succeed in spite of them.

A subtle hunter.

              Like the peregrine
              who, enthroned on her thermals,
              circles her prey

                      unseen

                              unheard
              calibrating

                  windspeed

                        pressure
                rock dove velocity

              she focuses
              on the apex of its wings
                    which look to her
              as if they're a heartbeat away,
                  until

              she decides
                    that everything is right

she folds back her wings

and stoops
stoops

stoops

and with her talons foremost
strikes:

a kill.

I saw a deer drive once:
there was a team of lads and dogs
with Patrick in the glen
conducting them.

A chorus of shot.
The dogs driven on.
And a hind of the high hill
brought down.

PART TWO: MOVEMENT

Pibroch: *ceol mor*, the 'big music' of the Gaels.
Ground and movement are its theme and variation.
Ben Dorain is a pibroch.
Deer are the reed
through which the mountain is played.

The song is in the piper's view,
her fingers climb
not to a summit, but the plateau
where she stays for as long as she can.
Endurance as craft. Technique
as footsteps on the surface
of the possible.
Rivers and boulders,
heather, bracken, scree.
Phrases repeat. Ben Dorain
is a pibroch. The ground
is embellished to the limits of grace.

(Jorie Graham: *things can be adjacent
and adjacency
creates a glow of meaning*)

The piper walks out into the pibroch.
Sometimes she comes back to the ground.
Sometimes the song takes off
like a deer fleeing over the heath:

That little hind with the
                    face that tapers to
          an arrowhead

          is running   running

She's shrewd at reading the wind;
with her quick sure hooves and slender limbs
she ghosts over the slopes

and won't come down, for fear
of guns and men.
Though she's always running

you'll never see her out of breath:
          she has the vigour of her mothers.

Darwin:
those who nourish their offspring best
leave the greatest number to inherit
their superiority.

She pauses for a deep   draught of air
and then the pure bell of her voice

          rings out –

it fills me with joy, the season's lusty call
as she searches the hill for her lover,

the stag with the all-consuming roar.

John Luther Adams:
I no longer want to be outside
the music, listening
to it as an object apart.
I want to inhabit the music,
to be fully present and listening
in that immeasurable space.

White-rumped, wild-headed,
holding his many-branched antlers aloft,
he has beaten the bounds of the mountain
until he wears it
like a skin.

This is pure Ben Dorain,
republic of deer.

T.H. Clutton-Brock:
As a result of clearance
and enclosure, Scottish red deer
(historically used to woodlands of birch,
willow, alder and pine)
have been progressively
confined to open moorland.

Nimble-footed,
      birch-thin,
            a hind
with her calf in close pursuit.

Their white scuts
      are what you see first;

picking their way up the mountain pass,
over the edge of Harpist's Corrie.

When she stretches her limbs
     and runs with all her might
her hooftips hardly touch the earth

          – like the breath of the wind
          like the sky tremoring with starlings –

then who would catch her?
Could any man keep up?

A boisterous band of calves and hinds
play *king-o'-the-castle* and *tig-round-a-hillock*
racing in circles and changing direction,
doubling back and then racing in circles,

charging uphill
     and leaping stiff-legged

          a storm of brown leaves
          a swirl of elvers

no shadow
can settle
on their minds.

They're fickle, the hinds,

          like light on the hill

they're flirtatious,
ever-ready,
unweighted by sorrow or age.

Do you see their glossy coats and the firm flesh
from neck to rump?
Let me tell you their secret.

They know this land,
　　　　　they live it.
It's their trove, their commonground,

　　　　　　　　　　　from the high summer pasture
　　　　　　　　　　　to the shelters of winter
　　　　　　　　　　　they dwell where they will.

The hill is their mother,
it nurses the calves:

　　　　　　　　　　　hair-grass, woodrush, deer's hair,
　　　　　　　　　　　vernal, milkwort, sorrel,
　　　　　　　　　　　lichens, sedges, club moss,
　　　　　　　　　　　fringe moss, fescue, foxtails,
　　　　　　　　　　　wild thyme, chickweed,
　　　　　　　　　　　cushion moss.

The calves, with their speckled coats,
are joy itself, all fun and games

　　　not even the cold
　　　　　　　　　　　　　　　　subdues them
　　　　　　　these nimble ones
　　　　　　　　　　　　　　　with their
　　　　　　　　snuffling noses
　　　　　with their
　　　　　　　　　　　　　　　　　little white
　　　　　　　haunches
　　　　　　　　　　　　　　　They're as vital
　　　　as the fresh
　　　　　　　　　　　　　　stream water
　　　　　　　they drink
　　　　　　　　　　　　　　　　　You can hear
　　　them rustling
　　　　　　　　　　　　through glens
　　　　　　　　　　　　　　　　　of sweet grass

　　　　　　　　　　(shhhhhhhhhhhhhhhh)

And when the snow comes
they always find shelter in
the dell, their stronghold,
hidden among the high
rock-stacks. Here they lie
in safety, between the fairy
mounds,

near Ais an t-Sìthein,

my home.

PART THREE: HOME

I love to rise

                          as dawn's

     alighting

               on the sill,

that's when it's best

         to do a circuit of the hills:

Cold Hill first, or maybe Castle Hill,
then back across the strath to Monk's Hill,
down to Cairn Hill, Congregation Hill,
and the final pull over rugged slopes
to the hill of a thousand streams, Ben Dorain.

I'll count at least two hundred deer —
this is the place
where they ought to be,
my simple-minded ones,
        waking with light hearts,
        luminous with joy.

Listen!
        From their slender frames
resounds a great music,
the clear honest melody
of their distant calls:

a hind will stitch
        her voice into the wind,
a sharp staccato
        bark with intervals
of five to fifteen seconds.
        Her role is to warn
the herd of trouble — at her bark
        they're instantly alert.

The leader carries the tune
    alone, no other member
of the herd joins in
    with this salute,
this gathering song,
    this retreat.

It's a special sound, when they start
    with their keening and crooning.
I'd take it
over all the music of the Gaels
    this sweet song
        this breath
passed down through generations,
this ardent belling
    on the face of Ben Dorain

(but look down there,
at the fussy grey hind
wallowing in the pool
while her herd bark –
she has funny ways, that girl,
when the mood takes her).

Do you hear that stag with the distinctive roar
hauled from the fathoms of his chest?
When he strikes up
you hear him in the next glen –

    he roars
    roaringly, he can roar
    no other way;
    the world
    is its own
    true self in him.

The young hind with the sweet lowing voice
leads her calf up the scree-slope;
                    they call to each other
                    across that great
longing of mother and child.

The stag's vision is sharp,
his quick gaze steady
as he portions up the glen;
below his grey eyebrows,
beneath lashes and lids,

                                        are pupils
                                        as remote
                                        from me
                                        as Jupiter.

He's a trooper, that one
who runs on ahead
with the vigour of a newly-kindled fire:

                    you're sure of yourself
                    no falter in your step
                    no restraint in your leap
                    in the race of your being
                    there's no second place
            you sprint onward and onward
                    without glancing backward
            and no one, two-legged or four,
                    can keep up

                            over
                    rough water   rugged water   narrow water
                                coarse water

over burns
that flash
and
twist
like otters
the stag
leaps

over
stony water   strong water   harsh water
              fricative water

The hind is browsing on the heath,
her land of plenty:
heath rush and tufted club-rush,
robust young herbs
to put fat on your flanks –

a clump of bristles, a small sweep's brush;
a bouquet of fibre optic cables.

To her that mountain spring
is sweeter than Sauternes,
than Tokaji. It's a well of fresh green shoots
at which she'll drink   drink

             drink

                drink
             drink.

Ben Dorain breathes   through its rivulets,
those constant, descending scales
from ridge
             to face
                  to moor
to the calm of the strath.

But the hillweaving herd have other lines.
They follow them up and down the slopes,
as the piper traverses
                    her pentatonic range.

There are deer paths as old
as those Ice Age pioneers
who browsed the tundra
of the Dogger Bank, antlers
long since submerged by the rising sea.

Their paths lead over slopes marked
                    by piss and oestrus,
                    by the stink of the rut.

Their paths lead past the patch
where the stag, whose testes have swelled
in response to the long summer days,
is unsated in his rutting:
                    he runs an antler
                    through the grass
                    as gently as
                    a lover's caress,
                    as gently
                    as the hind
                    nuzzling
                    her calf,
                    until, in a minute or so,
                    he ejaculates
                    into the grass.

Their paths lead to rubbing trees and wallows.
Their paths lead round bogs
where the horseflies hatch.
Their paths lead to the land
where the forage is sweetest.

Field grass, freshly scythed,
is not for you. You prefer
the sedge and sorrel of the moor;

your tastes are for primrose,
St John's wort,
tormentil's yellow lobes,
tender spotted orchids
whose flowerheads cluster
on the meadow, spiked
and forked and glossy.

These are the delicacies of the hill,
the diet to brace you for winter:
across your back there's a roll of fat,

and yet
you'll never be less than light on your feet.

When a deer lacks calcium, say, or phosphorus,
this is manifested as appetite: food that's rich in
calcium or phosphorus tastes better as a result.
Hence, cast antlers are eaten. Hence, the ribs
and skull of another deer (its carcass cleaned by
crow and raven, eagle, pine marten, the larvae of
muscid flies, teams of sexton beetles) are eaten.
And the earth slowly pulls down what remains
into its dark, quiet, underlying life.

Sweetness to a deer is a food that's rich in mineral salts. Plants that grow high on mountain slopes are sweeter than plants that grow on peat. In winter, deer prize the club moss revealed by thawing snow. In summer they graze the peat-free hilltops.

During daylight hours they avoid the green slopes on which their red coats are most visible. But as the light fades they are drawn to these places...

At dusk,
   as the last
  faint glaze of light
hangs over the cobalt hills

they are there
in the hollow
at the foot
of the mountain

   this fellowship
  of calves and hinds,
  graceful,
intimate:

however long the night
no harm will come to them.

This simple home
   with its generous table
is where they belong;

on the moor
        in the mountains
                they make their beds.

The rich colour of their pelts
        brings me joy – they knew
what they were doing, those stags
        who first made Ben Dorain their own.

PART FOUR: MYTH

Turn back a page in the register of time
and read an earlier inscription

(raven quill   oak apple ink
a monk   a vellum margin)

     the sunlight
     through the willow leaves
     flickers over my page
     and brings me joy

An instant, brought
continually into being.
A scribe's humble art.
A man who, like Duncan Bàn,
is swept off his feet by the world:

Mountain of herbs and saplings

mountain of hummocks and hillocks

mountain of superabundance

     in your green summer robe
     you're the finest in the world.

Laden with gifts, abounding with fruits:
the green berries of the glen
always ripen on your slopes —
I can't believe that the records reserve
first place for other, lesser bens.

In full Highland dress, jewelled with woods,
each thicket waving its blossoms in the wind,
you're flawless, Ben Dorain, you lack nothing.

Walk into the text at a different point,
before the hills were overstocked with deer
for sport and profit; before the poet
watched sheep lay them to waste;
before progress, with its stocks and shares,
turned Duncan and his people from the land;
before bare slopes and heather
were branded *timeless wilderness.*

The proud cockerel
                    pushes out his chest
                                        and –

you know how it goes,
the recital's well polished.

Around him smaller birds
build their shieling of song:

            each anthem declares "I am"
            each antiphon "I belong".

There's a nifty wee buck,
a virtuoso on the hill,

he never slips, never comes a cropper,
he jinks over the slopes like a flying winger:

he ranges through corries,
sure-footed, well-antlered –
come heather, come high ground,
he climbs for the hell of it –
through bracken and brushwood
he freestyles, he wanders –
at the foot of each gully,
on the height of each hillock,
he's playful, he's vital,
long-strided, elusive –

he's a maestro, fluent in his medium.

He performs the hill
with every scratch and scat and wallow,
　　　　at every heartbeat;
when at rest
he dreams the bank of watercress and vetch,
the boulder, the cloud of clegs.

His hooves riff and glissando
on the rocks. He knows by heart
the trill of morning birchwood,
the flutes and clarinets and horns
of the ridge, the water's
themes and variations,
each one part of the pibroch of the hill.

But for the buck
        a broken twig
                        a flash
            an unknown scent
an unfamiliar point on the horizon

is a note
in the chorus of fear
he can never sing, and never
stop hearing.
This is being a deer.

When he's startled in the wood
he doesn't pause, he doesn't hesitate,
he races through thickets of hazel,
a sprinter, a champ. He runs

and time
collapses
to one
adren-
alised
moment;
blood
diverts
from gut
to legs;
his frame
is taut
as drumskin

his slender hooves make
        thistledown strides
as he gallops over mounds
        of dead brown moss

and his mind soon turns
to lust for a hind,
his body longs
for rut.

That small hind there,
all day she grunts and grumbles
to her young

(and in them are woven
those ancient threads
intimacy
and fear)

ears swivel, primed to listen;
her eyes scan the hills, a lookout;
she's got hooves she can trust
to carry her over the moors.

Bring on the Gaelic heroes of old,
bring on Caoilte the quick, the man
who runs with the sureness of a buck,
who can speak the tongue
of every living thing;

bring on Cuchulainn, son of the storm,
warrior wilder than any dog,
fury of the fight itself;

and while you're at it, bring on
all the horses and men of King George:

unless her skin is torn
by the first lead shot,
there's no-one on earth
who will take her alive

she runs into the margins of time's book,
where words and landscape fuse
in an ecology of myth:

look as she joins the four red stags
who gnaw at the shoots of Yggdrasil

look as her heart's torn out on the Steppe
and the shaman rides her soul
to the otherworld

look at Cernunnos the virile god
the horned one, the Celtic god of the wild

look as St Kentigern
yokes her to a plough
taming wildness in the name of God

look at her lying with the terracotta troops
ears pricked for the noise of the hunt
in the emperor's next life.

Turn away in fear
as she glides through the wood's holy dark,
Artemis and her golden hind

turn away as the Choctaw deer-woman
lures young men into a trap
of their own lust

turn away as Saraswati, river of wisdom,
Brahma's creative power,
puts on her hooves, her pelt
as red as the first rays of the sun

The hind is spry
she's eccentric   capricious   strong-willed
white-rumped   long-legged   stump-tailed

        (she's as
          hard
        to sound
           as
       Rannoch's
         peat-
         black
        pools)

she runs from our dogs
as her mothers ran from wolves –

no matter how steep
she keeps to the hills –

tossing her head, she's the petulant
queen of the high moor,
fretful and vigilant, sullen, far-sighted –

the threads of her life
the lines of her
becoming
compose this land:

like all her kin she's part
of the tapestry of the hill.

PART FIVE: COLOUR

Not the sound of a river
but the slow seep through grass and air,
the slip of boots on wet stone.

In the cloud's collapsed tent
the hillside is vinyl
revolving after the music has stopped,

the needle lifting back to the cradle.
Half-seen: a red hide. A shattering
of hooves, bounding off —

She's always in motion, this doe,
                                  like a stream
like a flame through the undergrowth.
Her bolthole's a bank of saplings.
She savours heather shoots
and soft leaves newly drawn
from the sheath of a bud;
she never lowers herself
to fodder.

And her temperament?
Meek, but airy-headed;
giddy, joyful. She's the rashest
and daftest of the herd:
you could say she plays the fool.

Sweet, shy creature,
you always find
        a haven
                in the hollow
with the greenest birch,
the most succulent dell.

Elusive poem
of a deer,
                moving in
        and out of vision;
my yearning
    for a place that's out of reach,
the articulable earth
of Duncan Bàn –
the sung water, land and sky,
            all their inhabitants.

She browses by the big crag;
all week long it is her idyll.

        (the bushes where she sleeps
        are her windbreak, they keep
        the merest breath from her.

        She's enfolded in the wood,
        nestled up against
        the rock that's called 'The Nose',

        in the midst of the brush
        among the alcoves of the hill).

Imagine
    you've spent hours walking the mountain,
    deeper and deeper in
    until you've come to know its paths,
    its rocks and burns, its deer trails,
    as well as you know the surface of the leaf
    held all day between finger and thumb,
    while in your boots your feet are hot,
    each step like treading on briars, the sweat
    on your face is dried to a layer of salt,
    and the twenty-year ache
    in your knee has roused from its slumber
    so that when you rest your legs shiver.
    In the village that night,
    you sit with the first cold pint before you
    like a whole world:

that's how deeply the doe drinks
from the great spring, high on the southern slopes.
This is the brew for her,
that keeps her healthy
             unconstrainable
                  forever young:
she's swift in a crisis —
         with her balletic
chase and turn
she eludes any hunters.

Look out for her, a lithe red form
with a hint of asphodel to her pelt.

To describe the virtues that combine in her
I'd be a painter
using all the colours on my palette.

But she's tough – she can handle the cold
and is peerless for pace.
I can't believe she has an equal.

                                          And as I walk

                       this deer

                                 this hill

                 think themselves within me:

                             not   river

                                  slow   air

                           slip

                             cloud's

                                  vinyl

                        revolving

                                  lifting   to the
                                red

                                    off

PART SIX: RUT

Years later
I still think of them:
glorious

                                        a gallus team
                                        striding forth
                                        in the flesh
                                        of the moment

assembling
                to jostle and clatter
                                up the cliffs —

between the moor with the naked birch
and the mouth of Fortress Corrie

they carry themselves like lords

                outside commerce
                outside property law
                the land is theirs
                and they serve it.

This is their paradise, enclosed by hills.
They wander up the sides of Bracken Corrie,
thread through the pass
to the field of hard water,
the plain we used to call
Wolf's Garden.

They browse at Willow Crag,
roam the northern slopes
where two ridges run
together like the cloven
halves of a hoof.

On the high moor

                              where the autumn tides of grass
                              usher in the rut

the hinds are parading –

                              a matriarchal tribe
                              who tolerate the stags
                              for six weeks in a year.

The thrill of the season is on them

                              the stag is hefted
                              to a moving territory,
                              his harem in the hills;

they sport with each other,
        bound over moorland and moss

                              when a hind strays,
                              the stag brings her back;
                              when she slows
                              he lowers his head and tries
                              to lay his coarse chin on her rump.
                              Too early in oestrus.
                              She races off.

            They charge through bogs –

                              he rakes the ground
                              one antler at a time
                              and pisses in the wallow pool;
                              he fills his lungs
                              with its buttery

citric musk; he rolls
until his coat and the earth
and the whole glen (if he could)
are penetrated
with his presence.

She becomes aroused

the stag, like a master of wine,
noses her vulva,
takes a sip of her
on his tongue,
draws back his upper lip
to better taste
her readiness.

They're a carnival of desire.

He licks her head, her neck,
the base of her tail.
She rubs her whole length
along his ribs,
working towards his rear
until she makes
to mount him.

Ben Dorain hosts
    a bacchanal:

now he mounts her
    she stands

he mounts her
    she stands

he mounts her
    she stands

he mounts her
  she stands

in the infinity
  of herself,
the countless inter-
  woven trails
of all that she is:
  gladness, lust,
the scents of rut,
  textures of fur
and grass in the gut,
  pebble in a hoof,
iron in the blood,
  the weight of the stag
as he mounts and thrusts.

At last she'll stand
  in the queerness
of pregnancy,
  one body
antlering into two.

The part of us that's deer
satisfies its thirst

on the slopes below Congregation Hill
where Annat Burn (the stream
of the chapel of an unknown saint)
brings its heather-honeyed water,
the hill's holy wine,
into the glen,

glistening

        gushing

               quickening

filtering as it flows
over its gravel bed,
sweeter than cinnamon
richer than cloves.

Sometimes, Duncan Bàn, you'd think
that you couldn't sleep
without the whispering songs
of the burns of Ben Dorain,
the soft red noise of your soul;

but for more than half your life

you heard only carts on cobbled
streets, the curfew beat
upon guardsmen's drums,
the endless repeating
anthems of economic growth.

Annat rises deep inside the earth,
      a never-failing tonic,
        abundant wealth
that can't be traded.

It flows between the arms
of the land's most majestic hills:

                              listen
                    the clear-
              flowing

        water
              gentle-
                    flavoured
                              clear-
              headed
              water
                    bubbling and
                              surging its
                        way down
                              hill from the
                              shady
                              springs

    thamnobryum alopecurum   nestled in   foxtail feather-moss
    maidenhair pocket-moss   water-   *fissidens adianthoides*
    cratoneuron filicinum   cress   fern-leaved hook-moss
    wry-leaved tamarisk-moss   liverworts   *heterocladium heteropterum*
    conocephalum salebrosum   moss   great-scented snakewort

            lean in and imagine you're carving a path
                through this inch-high holy grove
        where distinctions collapse in the shifting light, where
            everything radiates everything else

The eddying pool
on the shoulder of Ben Dorain

is the pellucid music

of a chorus of bells:

    weightless

        melody

          of water

            ringing out

                the silver

                    tongues

            of countless

                burns

                    the larks

            and the wings

                of mining bees

                    landing

            on yellow

                flowers

                    madrigals

            vespers

                of the Ben

                    the piper's ground

            embellished

                and forever

                    coming into being:

Land of ditch and dell
hump and hillock
pillar and precipice

ruffled as the sea   rough-coated as a stag

matted with shoots and pastures of grass,
ganglia, cortex of steep, tufted paths

and the noses, eyes, ears
of the hill, tooth, talon and wing,
croziers, spikelets, radicles, roots,
the great breaths of day and night

blossoming budbursting flowerblushing hill:
lightdappled greenmantled lifebuzzing hill:

from the heights of its slopes to the heart of its plains
this deer-land is decked
with riches with branches with creatures
with the world
thrumming through it —

PART SEVEN: WEB

With my feet and my lungs
I think the ground's contours:

> bare rock   high slopes
> soft hollows   heather corries

The germinating hill
murmurs gentleness to calves,
to stags with their antlers hardening
at bramble time

> Ben Dorain   past and future mountain
> cast your net   of possible selves:

On the sun-soaked southern flanks
   the young hind and her echo-footed stag luxuriate,
married by weather and world

> rockface quartz   layers of schist
> garnet   semipelite
> the bedrock   the hidden heart
> sedimentary   metamorphic

She's in her fertile prime – fat reserves
   for winter, glossy coat, calm temperament.
Breath of meadow grass and milkwort

> bent grass   tufted hair grass
> cotton grass   purple moor grass

This is Heather Corrie.
Those who know it well
love it in the ways
of rowan, alder, ptarmigan

           fur on thorn   pellet of short-eared owl
           rabbit skull   crumbling sheiling wall

High on the ridge
      the wind
leans in and blows
      through fluted
crevices,
      the chanter of the hill

           magpie moth   mountain ringlet
           northern eggar   northern dart

           emperor moth   green tiger beetle
           heath bumblebee   four-spotted chaser

The music of the wind-gaps
      summons forth
the lads of the glen,
      drawing them
to the slopes where they know
      the herd will be,
where their mortal songs
      ring out
on gun barrel pipes

sheep grazing   moor burning
barbed wire   soil erosion

railway curled   round the western slopes
viaduct   A82

estate roads   grouse butts
winter deer food   (micronized wheat cubes)

crane flies   sheep ticks
black slugs   deer flies

turbines   superquarries
pylons   hydro lochs

conifer forest   conifer forest
conifer forest   conifer forest
conifer forest   conifer forest
conifer forest   conifer forest

What other wealth is there
than that which is drawn out by the dew:
scents of dogrose and wild raspberry?

tormentil   bog asphodel
round-leaved sundew   starry saxifrage

roseroot   juniper
devil's-bit scabious   thrift

a hundred names   each one
a narrative   in bud

crowberry   bell heather
butterwort   creeping azalea

The deerslopes teem with tender leaves
and we in turn draw our food
from the teeming river

     herding the night-
     fished ones
     by torch
     towards
     the great
     roaring

     where pine-
     sharp spears
     are held in
     grinning fists

wildcat   grey wolf
pine marten   brown bear

In calm pools the unhunted trout
harvest flies and larvae,
their flitting plenty

litany   cartography
topogeny   potentiality

Darwin's entangled bank
MacDiarmid's "Scotland small?"

Ruskin's Crossmount studies
Blake's world in a grain of sand

You are more opulent than sea or wood.
You are no wilderness.

PART EIGHT: EMERGENCE

Amergin, mythic bard who strode
from coracle to shore, chanting the Celtic earth,
its flowerings, fruitings, moultings,
entangle us in the present
of your song, the emergent world:

> I am the wind ranging over the sea
> I am wave and ocean, climate systems
> I am the charge in a circuit board
>
> I am elm and heather, aspen, alder
> I am hawkweed, hybridising
> I am the root and aril of the yew
>
> I am hookworms, pinworms,
> whipworms, rhizomes, spores
> I am herbivore and apex predator
>
> I am the subsoil superstrings
> of honey fungus, the wood's leviathan
> I am hazelnut and slow worm's scales
>
> I am rust on pit wheels and dockyard cranes
> I am peregrines perching on a towerblock roof
> I am lace-workers stitching in air
>
> I am the hunter downwind among the rocks
> I am the hind fearing footsteps on the wind
> fearing bullets and blood and terror and dogs

It takes skill to stalk a deer,
        a flair for patience
bordering on witchcraft
        (earache from the winter wind;
frozen hands that hold
        a gun for three hours
as you wait for her to stand).

I am the glacier of cloud flooding the glen
I am Pangea, Laurentia, Afro-Eurasia
I am the hyperobjectivity of the hill

She's alone —
        approach her at the pace
that eggshell thickens,
        that berries ripen
among the thorns.
        Work your way
through cover.
        If she's spooked, if she
raises her head
        and you're not invisibly
still, if she lowers
        her head again but out
of the corner of her eye
        she sees you breathe,
if she scents a single
        pheromone of you,
she's gone.

Do you take the land into
yourself, or does the land receive
you further into it?

I am the world as sharp as an adder's tooth

Rethink knowledge:
      not information, not even
sense data.
      Knowing the hill
means prone legs drawn
      into the dampening earth.
It means peat in your hair,
      your boots, your lungs.
Negotiate each pit
      and fold, each clump,
each tuft of grass.
      Your knee
stiffens on cold stone.

Heraclitus: *each individual thing comes out of the one,*
and the one comes out of each thing

You open door
      after door until
you can go
      no further.
Taste of bilberry
      and bracken.
Memories of boulders,
      their angles
of concealment.
      Cartography
of clouds;
      shadows moving
over the earth.
      Body
and land, air
      and mind,
close on each other:

plant and human
stone and bird
are one weave, one plaid.

If you're humble
there's a chance
that in spite
of their best efforts,
you will kill a deer.

Fix	your resolute	rewilded
eye	on a stag	Gather
to you	all your threads	of instinct
experience	skill	Steer the long-
barrelled	trickster	the glutton
(coyote	raven	*am bòcan*)
at the heart	of the running	mountain
Rest the inner	joint	of a finger
on the trigger –	mechanism	poised
to pounce	to lash out	at your will
(yes yours	dear reader	dear hunter
for meaning	for order)	prime
mover	destroyer	of worlds

The fresh flint in the hammer –

is about to strike the plate.

the talon of the gun –

The mountain draws its breath.
The deer, the mice, the sphagnum
draw breath. Teeming soil
of beetles and bacteria.

We are here in this place
between one moment
and the next. A fly is held
mid-buzz. Antlers turn
in the light.

Sparks catch the crisp powder
nestled behind the shrivelled tinder.
They bring forth flames and a deadly hail,
the song of my prima donna of the hills.

She's an ardent messenger, a grave ambassador:

        impact

        comes

        before

        she is

        heard

the bullet pierces hide and
stomach, lung, shatters
rib and shoulder, finds
out every corner.
One by one each mystery
of living matter
is uncovered.

Now blood on heather.
It seeps from the wounds
of the long-limbed
        nimble-mouthed
              staggering
children of the hills.

Walk again to where
the hill first rises from the glen
(this is not an image
to admire from distance, a static
scene to hang upon a wall):

The herd lies down
on the slopes around Willow Crag,
the place that is their knowledge –

aesthetics, science, psychology,
the great tradition
of meadow grass, deer path, wallow pool.

To drive them from it
is violence. You won't clear them
from their learning
without a show of force

(the shaping of the land
implied in 'landscape').

What you need is a braying pack.

For the hind the only sound that matters now
is neither wind nor pipes nor the melodies of birds

but the snarl of dogs.
She is frenzied, shell-shocked.

I am shantytown tarpaulin, the imprisoned child
I am the family burning in their Sutherland home
I am typewriters and bodies bulldozed into graves

And it's a thrill to those chaps
who know their sport and still
have all the virility of youth,
who love the freedom of the hills

which they imagine are inert
or all the same.

Loudly the deer stir.
Sleepless the men chase.
Guns are ready to bestow their gifts.

With each man there's a dog, consumed
by the duty and joy of the hunt:

> a swaggering warrior, powerful and potent;
> malicious and keen as a missile, impatient;
> surly, forbidding, boorish and sinister;
> yapping and yowling at the work he was bred for;
> brows bushy, jaws open, hackles erect,
> he quivers and shudders, is murder incarnate.

The drive is a tidal wave –
a headlong pursuit
unpredictable.

Echoes bay for blood.
The sons and daughters of the rock
answer back with their baying.

A shaggy-headed hound calls out.
He forces the herd from their high havens.

Hooves try to fathom the depths of the hill,
its hidden tracks, its shortcuts,

> but there are pools too deep
> for a deer to sound.

A hind drags the torn
gown of herself
into the surge.

                                        She looks up into eyes
                                        other than her own.

The pack charge on
and another hind
is seized by the throat —

another and another, each
in her own grief

                                        like a clifftop stream falling
                                                into the sea
                                        like a spark thrown out
                                                from the peats
                                                to the stone hearth.

Always the clamour of the hunt.

There is too much.

I can't give the deer
all that is their due.

I have tried
                and now the words
                        slip away

        all that's left are the songlines of the hill

                its typeface of lichen and stone

                the semantics of the thousand tones

                of fast and deep and shallow burns

water seeping into hoofprints

wind filling a raven's wings

wasps chewing bark from the heather

a hare pressing into moss

a moth settling on a leaf

the breathing shapes of deer

II

RO-RÀDH

Meg Bateman

Tha *Moladh Beinn Dòbhrain* air fear de na dàin as annasaiche a th' againn sa Ghàidhlig – gu dearbha, tha e air fear de na rudan as annasaiche sa chultar air fad. Cha ghabh e creidsinn ciamar a chaidh dàn anns a bheil còrr is 550 sreath a chur ri chèile – no fiù 's a chur air chuimhne – gun chothrom air sgrìobhadh agus an structar iom-fhillte a' gluasad eadar ùrlar is siubhal agus a' crìochnachadh le crùnludh. Tha eòlas mionaideach a' bhàird air na fèidh fhèin na annas gu leòr.

Tha seasamh an dàin àraidh cuideachd oir cuiridh e tuigse an cèill air co-eisimeil gach creutair agus lusa san àrainneachd fada mus robh am facal "eag-eòlas" againn. Agus, ged a mhìnicheas Donnchadh Bàn beatha nam fiadh air a' bheinn le bàigh is seirc, tha e comasach air labhairt air am bàs san t-seilg gun uabhas no truas. Bheir e an aon spèis dhan t-sealgair agus innleachdas a' ghunna 's a bheir e dha na fèidh oir, dhàsan, tha àite aig mac-an-duine san àrainneachd cuideachd, dìreach mar a tha aig na fèidh, na lusan, na h-eòin agus na h-èisg.

Seach gum bi Beinn Dòbhrain a' toirt àrach do dh'uiread de rudan beò, chì Donnchadh Bàn mar mhàthair i ann an trusgan nan lus, is e a' tarraing air miotas nan Gàidheal. Cha b' ann gus an 20mh linn a chleachd James Lovelock ìomhaigh na mnà a-rithist na *Gaia Hypothesis* agus e a' tuigsinn na Cruinne-Cè mar chorp beò anns am bi buaidh aig gach ball air slàinte na h-uile.

Tha beartas cànan an dàin a' dol na mheatafor air beartas na h-àrainneachd fhèin, agus na dhà dhiubh, gach sreath den dàn is gach dùil bheò, a rèir choltais comasach air ath-nuadhachadh gun cheann. A bharrachd air sin, tha ceòl an dàin (oir 's e òran a th' ann) a' dol na mheatafor air co-sheirm nàdair.

Chan eil bàs na h-èilde na uabhas aig an deireadh a chionn 's gu bheil èildean eile ann: tha cothromachd na h-àrainneachd fhathast ann.

Ma tha ath-aithris aig a' bhàrd a thaobh nam fiadh, chan eil an sin ach samhail air an dol-a-mach aca is iad a' dìreadh is a' teàrnadh nan stùc, a' sireadh luibhean àraidh is a' gairm air a chèile. Tha nàdar làn ath-aithris gun tùs no èis.

Canaidh Donnchadh Bàn, *Tha an eilid anns an fhrìth / mar bu chòir dhi bhith* agus tionndaidhidh e iomadh uair gu ceist còir nam beathaichean agus nan daoine air Beinn Dòbhrain, is e a' tarraing a-rithist air miotas nan Gàidheal anns am bi an talamh agus mac-an-duine gu torrach pòsta aig a chèile, is iad a' meudachadh piseach agus rath a chèile. Ann an dàn eile, *Òran nam Balgairean*, nì e gearan gu bheil a' Ghàidhealtachd air fàs *mì-nàdarra* às dèidh fuadachadh an t-sluaigh.

> Tha h-uile seòl a b' àbhaist
> > anns a' Ghàidhealtachd air caochladh,
> Air cinntinn cho mì-nàdarra
> > sna h-àitean a bha aoigheil.

Dha rèir-san, tha àite aig mac-an-duine ann an nàdar is chan e àite gun daoine a th' ann idir, mar a chìte ri linn Romansachais e.

Bha Donnchadh Bàn air uabhasachadh aig deireadh a bheatha nuair a thill e a dh'Earra-Ghàidheal às dèidh dha a bhith ag obair na fhreiceadan an Dùn Èideann. Rinn e *Cumha Coire a' Cheathaich* is e a' caoidh mar a bha an àrainneachd air dhol a dholaidh a chionn 's nach robh cùram aig duine dha na na coilltean is na h-uillt. Mar thoradh air seo, bha na fèidh – teachdairean na talmhainn – air teicheadh. Bha an t-eag-shiostam air dhol bho ghleus. Bha nàdar a' fulang, na bheachd-san, às aonais stiùbhartachd mic-an-duine.

> 'S e 'n coire chaidh an dèislaimh
> On a tha e nis gun fhèidh ann,
> Gun duin' aig a bheil spèis diubh
> > Nì feum air an cùl.

A dh'aindeoin mothachadh a' bhàird dhan dàimh seo eadar "eag-eòlas" nàdair agus mac-an-duine, sgrìobh Kurt Wittig mu bhàrdachd Ghàidhlig an 18mh linn, "Nature is valued solely because of the aesthetic delight which it affords; there is no philosophical reflexion on it, no pantheism" (*The Scottish Tradition in Literature*, 1958, 194). A bharrachd air sin, sgrìobh Angus Macleod, neach-deasachaidh Dhonnchaidh Bhàin, "If in poetry we require sublimity of thought, a philosophy of life or compelling emotion, we shall find Duncan Macintrye wanting" (*Orain Dhonnchaidh Bhàin*, 1978, xl). A chionn 's gu bheil an fheallsanachd air a filleadh a-steach san ìomhaigheachd, an e nach deach a faicinn am broinn drilseachd nam facal? An e gun robh am bàrd fhathast air thoiseach air feallsanachd nàdair san 20mh linn? 'S dòcha nach e *feallsanachd* ach *sealladh* am facal ceart, ga chur an cèill tro mheatafor a' chiùil thar nan uile, is gach rud beò ann an co-sheirm ri Beinn Dòbhrain.

Eu-coltach ri Macleod agus Wittig, tha Garry MacCoinnich air leth mothachail air sealladh a' bhàird agus mar a tha an dàn a' cur ri deasbad na h-àrainneachd nar latha-ne. Ma mheasas cuid gun robh Donnchadh Bàn na dhuine soineanta sìmplidh, tha MacCoinnich na chaochladh is e foghlamaichte feòrachail. Tha e do-dhèante nach toireadh e an aire dha teagsaichean eile gus cur ris an eòlas aige air teachd-air-tìr nam fiadh. Ma bhios an sealladh aig Donnchadh Bàn falaichte ann am briathrachas, structar agus ceòl an dàin, tha ciall MhicCoinnich a' tighinn am follais gu h-eadar-theagsail eadar faclan Dhonnchaidh is na faclan aige fhèin is aig càch. Tha e air dhol an sàs ann an còmhradh ri iomadh taobh den dàn aig Donnchadh Bàn agus saoilidh mi gu bheil e air dàn a cheart cho dìomhair drùidhteach a chruthachadh. Tha na h-ùrlaran aig Donnchadh air dhol nan siùbhlaichean aig MacCoinnich.

Tha iomadh coimeas is sgaradh rin dèanamh eatarra. Air nòs Alasdair mhic Mhaighstir Alasdair, thagh Donnchadh Bàn cruth coltach ri ceòl mòr gus, 's dòcha, cearcallachd is caochlaideachd nàdair a riochdachadh. Ach 's e cruth ùr a dhealbhaich MacCoinnich: còmhradh ri leughadh ann an dà cholbh bho bhàrr gu bonn na duilleige, agus faclan Dhonnchaidh air an eadar-theangachadh air an taobh chlì agus na smuaintean aige fhèin air an taobh dheas. Aithnichear ruitheaman Dhonnchaidh Bhàin san eadar-theangachadh ach uaireannan tha na faclan a' dol nam bàrdachd nitheil is iad a' riochdachadh nan èildean is am mean a' sgaoileadh thar an t-slèibh no allt a' ruith eadar diofar sheòrsachan de chòinneach. Mar Dhonnchadh Bàn, tha MacCoinnich gu trom an sàs ann am meatafor a' chiùil. 'S e an talamh na dosan agus na fèidh an rìbheid a sheinneas port a tha an dà rud àrsaidh (a chionn 's gun robh na fèidh air Beinn Dòbhrain bho linn na dèighe) agus ùr (a chionn 's gu bheil iad òg). Airson an dà bhàird, bidh na fèidh, na h-eòin, a' ghaoth, na h-uillt agus fiù 's na mialchoin agus an gunna a' dèanamh co-sheirm anns a bheil barrachd is suim nam pàirtean.

Tha torrachas nàdair a' drùidheadh air MacCoinnich mar a dhrùidh e air a' bhàrd a bu shine (agus air Dylan Thomas anns "The force that through the green fuse drives the flower"). Ma chuireas Donnchadh Bàn seo an cèill tro laomsgaireachd nan lusan, cuiridh MacCoinnich an cèill e tro sgairtealachd is feòlmhorachd dàir nam fiadh. Chuir sìol an daimh a' spreadhadh air an fheur *Antichrist* le Lars von Trier air chuimhne dhomh is na daraich a' caitheamh nam mìltean de dhuircean às nach fhàsadh ach craobh no dhà.

Ged a bhios MacCoinnich a' cur earrannan fiosrachail ris an dàn (air fèidh ag ithe chnàmhan nuair a bhios iad gann de chailc, air litreachas nan Gàidheal no eachdraidh-beatha Dhonnchaidh Bhàin), tha cuspair a bharrachd air sin ann, ged nach eil iad buileach sgaraichte. 'S e sin, miann a' bhàird a bhith a' faicinn rudan mar a tha iad gun eadar-mhìneachadh na h-inntinn, rud a tha furasta dha fèidh is doirbh dha mac-an-duine. Seo an iargain a th' air a' bhàrd nuair a labhras e mun damh a tha a shùil cho fada bhuaithe ri Iupatar: *the world is its own true self in him.* Chan eil e ag iarraidh rudan fhaicinn mar a tha e a' smaoineachadh orra fa leth ach mar a tha iad ann am fìorachd is gach rud eile a' bualadh orra. (Nach e *phenomenology* a chanar ri seo?) Tha feallsanachd a' ruith tron dàn is sinne air ar dùsgadh dhi le às-earrannan à Spinoza, Thomas A. Clark is Heraclitus a dh'aithnich an ceangal eadar an rud fa leth agus na h-uile. B'e seo amas iomadh sgoil miostachais, Neo-platonachas nam measg, amas a tha soilleir ann an dualchas nan Gàidheal cuideachd. Nì MacCoinnich tarraing fhada air dàn am beul Amairgin, am bàrd a thàinig còmhla ris na Gàidheil às an Spàinn a dh'Èirinn, a rèir *Lebor Gabála*. Rinn e aonta le trì ban-diathan na h-Èireann às dèidh dha aonadh a dhèanamh ris an talamh, na beathaichean, ris a' ghaoith agus an t-sàl chun na h-ìre nach robh diofar eadar e fhèin is nàdar. Seo an t-aonadh a riochdaicheas an ceòl san dà dhàn. 'S dòcha gun cleachd MacCoinnich co-mhothachadh no *synesthesia* (nuair a bhios diofar cheudfathan a' dol am measg a chèile), gus plathadh dhe seo a chur an cèill, mar eisimpleir nuair a 'chì' e gairm na h-èilde na h-obair-ghrèis sa ghaoith.

Cha dèan Donnchadh Bàn iomradh air feallsanachd no feum à mòran ainmearan eas-cruthach, agus, mar a chunnacas gu h-àrd, chaidh a chàineadh le cuid airson dìth dhe leithid. Ach mar shealgair e fhèin, dh'fheumadh e a bhith cho eòlach air na fèidh 's gun robh e — mar Amairgin agus sealgairean Masai chun an latha an-diugh — cha mhòr a' dol na fhiadh e fhèin. 'S e an tuigse seo a tha cho àraidh mun dàn aige. Bruidhnidh e gu dìreach ris na fèidh agus ris a' bheinn is rudeigin den aon aonadh eatarra. Air a chaochladh, 's e an leughadair as trice a bhruidhneas MacCoinnich ris: *look with me / ... listen!*

Thug seann teags Gàidhlig eile, *Boile Shuibhne*, air bàrd eile, Rody Gorman, cruth ùr de bhàrdachd a chruthachadh ann an *Sweeney: an Intertonguing (a Subversion from the Irish)*. Tha e coltach gun robh tuigse aig na sean Ghàidheil air an àite aca fo chomhair nàdair as urrainn dhuinne a leughadh nar n-èiginn eag-eòlaich an-diugh mar shùileachan. Bruidhnidh Gorman às leth rìgh a b' fheàrr leis companas nan craobh, nam fiadh is na h-aibhne na gleadhraich na cùirte. Chithear a-cheana gun robh nàdar na spreigeadh gu cràbhachd nan Crìosdaidhean Gàidhealach tràtha seach na bhuaradh mar a bha e dha Augustine. Tha an dà bhàrd, MacCoinnich agus Gorman, cuideachd ag obair gu h-eadar-teagsail, is iad an sàs ann am measgachadh de dh'eadar-theangachadh agus de dh'obair chruthachail. Seach nach urrainn dhuinn smaoineachadh mar a smaoinich ar sinnsirean, nach eil e nas dìlse is nas onaraiche a bhith a' tighinn chun na h-obrach aca ler n-armachd inntleachdail fhèin — ar coimpiutairean a' cur thairis le fiosrachadh, ar n-imcheist air cion còrdaidh eadar ar dòigh-beatha is nàdar — is tnùth oirnn ri àite

where words and landscape fuse
in an ecology of myth.

Bu toigh le MacCoinnich an fhìorachd fhaicinn. Buinidh na fèidh is Beinn Dòbhrain ann an da-rìribh ri chèile; cha bhuin i dhan uachdaran ach greiseag agus sin a-mhàin ann am mac-meanmna mic-an-duine. Chan eil susbaint no brìgh air cùl a chòir air an talamh. Air còmhdach an leabhair, chithear dealbh de Bheinn Dòbhrain, na cruth suaimhneach coltach ri Fuji Yama, na seise dha gach beinn fon ghrèin. Ach san latha an-diugh 's e sgritheall is crotal a còmhdach seach an trusgan dosrach air an robh Donnchadh Bàn a-mach. Thig an dàn aig MacCoinnich gu crìch le seallaidhean luaineach air corra chreutair seach le crùnluth buadhmhor an t-sean bhàird. Tha Beinn Dòbhrain fhathast àlainn ach tha a nàdar againn air mhèidh.

An Lùnastal 2020, An t-Eilean Sgitheanach

INTRODUCTION

An Anglophone Version

Meg Bateman

Moladh Beinn Dòbhrain (Praise of Ben Dorain) by the eighteenth-century poet, Duncan Bàn MacIntyre, is one of the greatest marvels of Gaelic poetry – indeed it is one of the greatest marvels of the whole of Gaelic culture. It is hard to comprehend how without recourse to writing Donnchadh Bàn composed and remembered a poem of some 550 lines in a complex metre alternating, like a pibroch, between ground, variation and *crùnludh*. His minute observation of the deer and their habitat alone is marvel enough.

It is a mysterious poem with multiple ramifications. Donnchadh Bàn seems to have had an early understanding of the interrelatedness of different life forms long before the word "ecology" was coined. Thus, he is able to view the killing by the hunt of the deer that he has just so lovingly described without horror or sentimentality, because man and deer share the same environment and man eats the deer to survive. There are plenty other deer in the herd and the balance between life and death has been maintained. Man is part of nature, and as Iain Crichton Smith has pointed out, his gun and ingenuity at manufacturing and using it are praised by the poet as much as the agility of the deer. In understanding different species' adaptation to the environment, Donnchadh Bàn appears an early Darwinian too.

Ben Dorain's sustenance of various life forms – man, deer, birds, fish and vegetation – makes the hill a distinctly female presence in the poem. She is like a mother, dressed in the land's richly varied vegetation in the model of Gaelic mythology. It wasn't until the twentieth century that James Lovelock used the image of a woman again in his Gaia Hypothesis to communicate a sense of the Earth as an integrated living whole.

The richness of Donnchadh Bàn's language becomes a metaphor for the richness of nature, both seeming capable of endless variation and renewal. The poem is a song and the music itself becomes a metaphor for the co-existence of different forms of life. If there is some repetition in the poem describing the movement of the deer between their favourite pastures and their calling to one another as they ascend and descend the peaks, that is because there is repetition in nature.

Donnchadh Bàn says, *Tha an eilid anns an fhrìth / mar bu chòir dhi bhith (The hind is in the forest / as she ought to be)*. He alludes often to the right of animals and humans to Ben Dorain, drawing again on Gaelic mythology in which land and man form a union, each prospering the other. Human culture is part of nature and their communal and balanced existence creates harmonies of rich complexities. It is how the world is meant to be.

In a later poem, *Òran nam Balgairean (The Song of the Foxes)*, he goads the foxes to destroy the sheep that have replaced the people. He complains that the absence of people resulting from the Clearances is an unnatural state for the Highlands. He received a terrible shock towards the end of his life when he returned to Ben Dorain after working for many years in the city guard in Edinburgh and found that the mountain that he had taken as a symbol of immutability had indeed changed. In his song *Cumha a' Choire Cheathaich (Lament for the Misty Corrie)* he notes how with bad management, the corrie's forests and waterways have become clogged and the deer population – those avatars of the land – have fled.

How the corrie has gone to ruin,
since now it has no deer,
nor any man who loves them
and is efficient on their trail.

Donnchadh Bàn's view of intermeshing life forms and man's stewardship of nature – which have enormous implications for our present ecological crisis – seem to have been overlooked by earlier commentators. Kurt Wittig, writing of eighteenth-century Gaelic nature poetry, said, "Nature is valued solely because of the aesthetic delight which it affords; there is no philosophical reflection on it, no pantheism" (*The Scottish Tradition in Literature*, 1958, 194). Moreover, Donnchadh Bàn's editor, Angus Macleod, viewed him as naïve, albeit with a virtuosity for versification, stating, "If in poetry we require sublimity of thought, a philosophy of life or compelling emotion, we shall find Duncan Macintrye wanting" (*Orain Dhonnchaidh Bhain*, 1978, xl).

Garry MacKenzie however is acutely aware of the implications of the poem for our times. He is also aware of the impossibility of a writer today not working intertextually. MacKenzie is analytical and furthers his knowledge of the natural history of deer through study. If Donnchadh Bàn's stance is subsumed in the words, structure and music of the poem, MacKenzie's meaning literally appears intertextually, between his translation of Donnchadh Bàn and his own and others' writing. He has conversed with many aspects of the poem and has created another poem, I feel, of equal mystery and potency. Donnchadh's grounds have become MacKenzie's variations.

There are comparisons and contrasts to be made between MacIntyre and MacKenzie. While MacIntyre, following Alasdair mac Mhaighstir Alasdair (Alexander MacDonald), chose the form of the pibroch to mirror the variations and circularity of nature, MacKenzie has invented a new form: a conversation read from top to bottom of the page, but where left and right correspond to Donnchadh Bàn's translated lines and MacKenzie's reflections on them. We recognize the rhythms of the Gaelic in the translation but sometimes the columns blend as concrete poetry and the words scatter on the page like hinds and fawns on a hillside or like a burn tumbling down between a variety of mosses.

MacKenzie runs with the musical metaphor. The land plays the drones and the deer play the reed in a tune that is both ancient (because the deer have been on Ben Dorain since the end of the Ice Age) and new (because animal culture does not age like human civilisations). For MacIntyre and MacKenzie, the sounds made by the deer, birds, wind and burns, and even the hounds and the gun, sound together in harmony, and the whole is more than the sum of its parts.

Like Donnchadh Bàn, MacKenzie expresses the overwhelming fecundity of nature, the same force that Dylan Thomas sees in "The force that through the green fuse drives the flower". If Donnchadh Bàn expresses this through a wealth of plant and verse forms, MacKenzie expresses it in the vigour and sensuousness of the rutting of the deer. The stag ejaculating on the grass reminded me of the oak trees raining down acorns of which only one or two might become a tree in Lars von Trier's *Antichrist*.

In addition to MacKenzie's learned interjections (about deer eating bones when short of calcium, about Gaelic literature and details of Donnchadh Bàn's biography), there is another important subject raised in his poem. That is a longing for pure existence, for a perception of reality, not as a series of discrete objects perceived by the intellect but as experience perceived through the senses. The stag's perceptions are as far from the poet's as Jupiter in its ability to see things as they are: *The world / is its own / true self in him.* This philosophical strand sounds throughout the poem and we are wakened to it by quotations from Spinoza, Thomas A. Clark and Heraclitus. They recognise the interconnectedness of all things, the goal of many a school of mysticism including Neoplatonism, and part of Gaelic thinking too.

It isn't only the deer who are one and the same with what they perceive. MacKenzie quotes at length from Amairgin, the mythic poet of the Milesians who came with the first Gaels to Ireland according to *Lebor Gabála*. Amairgin, in making peace with the sovereignty goddesses of Ireland, achieves an identity with the land, beasts, wind and waves.

In both MacKenzie's and MacIntyre's poems, music represents the union of nature. It is also suggested by MacKenzie's use of synesthesia, by which, for example, he "sees" the call of the hind like lace in the wind. Donnchadh Bàn speaks directly to the deer and to the mountain, for – like Amairgin and the Masai hunters of today – he would have to sense being a deer himself to be able to track them. By contrast, MacKenzie mostly addresses a reader: *look with me / ... listen!*

It is interesting that another early Gaelic text, *Suibne Geilt* or *The Madness of Sweeney*, led another poet, Rody Gorman, to create a new form of translation, *Sweeney: an Intertonguing (a Subversion from the Irish)*. Clearly, the formulation of the Gaels regarding their relationship with nature makes sense to us today, in the midst of an ecological crisis. Gorman speaks on behalf of a king who preferred the company of trees, deer and a river to the bustle of the court. We see too that nature, viewed by Augustine as a distraction from the spiritual, was considered an incitement to piety among early Gaelic Christians. Both MacKenzie and Gorman work intertextually with a mixture of translation and creative response. Rather than attempting to reproduce the thinking of our ancestors, is it not more honest to come to their texts with our contemporary intellectual armour and concerns? Both poets have found a place

where words and landscape fuse
in an ecology of myth.

MacKenzie wants to see reality. The deer and Ben Dorain belong in reality to each other. Ben Dorain is only owned temporarily by a landlord and that only in the imagination of society. On the cover of the book there is a photo of Ben Dorain, "the equal of any mountain under the sun", its tranquil shape recalling Fuji Yama. But today its covering is scree and lichen rather that the luxuriant growth described by Donnchadh Bàn. MacKenzie's poem comes to an end with fleeting images of various creatures rather than with the majestic *crùnluth* of the older poem. Ben Dorain is still beautiful but its ecosystems of vegetation, deer and human society are not sounding together as they used to.

August 2020, Isle of Skye, Scotland

82

MOLADH BEINN DÒBHRAIN

Donnchadh Bàn Mac an t-Saoir

ÙRLAR

An t-urram thar gach beinn
   Aig Beinn Dòbhrain;
De na chunnaic mi fon ghrèin,
   'S i bu bhòidhche leam:
   Munadh fada rèidh,
   Cuilidh 'm faighte fèidh,
   Soilleireachd an t-slèibh
     Bha mi sònrachadh;
   Doireachan nan geug,
   Coill' anns am bi feur,
   'S foinneasach an sprèidh
     Bhios a chòmhnaidh ann;
   Greadhain bu gheal cèir,
   Faghaid air an dèidh,
'S laghach leam an sreud
     A bha sròineiseach.
'S aigeannach fear eutrom
   Gun mhòrchuis,
Thèid fasanda na èideadh
   Neo-spòrsail:
   Tha mhanntal uime fèin,
   Caithtiche nach trèig,
   Bratach dhearg mar chèir

Bhios mar chòmhdach air.
’S culaidh ga chur eug –
Duine dhèanadh teuchd,
Gunna bu mhath gleus
  An glaic òganaich;
Spor anns am biodh beàrn,
Tarrann air a ceann,
Snap a bhuaileadh teann
  Ris na h-òrdaibh i;
Ochdshlisneach gun fheall,
Stoc den fhiodh gun mheang,
Lotadh an damh seang
  Is a leònadh e;
’S fear a bhiodh mar cheàird
  Riutha sònraichte,
Dh’fhòghnadh dhaibh gun taing
  Le chuid seòlainean;
Gheibhte siud ri àm,
Pàdraig anns a’ ghleann,
Gillean is coin sheang,
  ’S e toirt òrdugh dhaibh;
Peileirean nan deann,
Teine gan cur ann;
Eilid nan àrd bheann
  Thèid a leònadh leo.

SIUBHAL

’S i ’n eilid bheag bhinneach
    Bu ghuiniche sraonadh,
Le cuinnean geur biorach
    A’ sireadh na gaoithe:
    Gasganach speireach,
    Feadh chreachainn na beinne,
    Le eagal ro theine
    Cha teirinn i h-aonach;
Ged thèid i na cabhaig,
    Cha ghearain i maothan:
    Bha sinnsireachd fallain;
    Nuair shìneadh i h-anail,
    ’S toil-inntinn leam tannasg
    Dha langan a chluinntinn,
’S i ’g iarraidh a leannain
    ’N àm daraidh le coibhneas.
    ’S e damh a’ chinn allaidh
    Bu ghealchèireach feaman,
Gu cabarach ceannard,
    A b’ fharamach raoiceadh;
’S e chòmhnaidh ’m Beinn Dòbhrain,
    ’S e eòlach ma fraoinibh.
’S ann am Beinn Dòbhrain,
    Bu mhòr dhomh r’ a innseadh
A liuthad damh ceannard
    Tha fantainn san fhrìth ud;
    Eilid chaol-eangach,
    ’S a laoighean ga leantainn,
    Len gasgana geala,
    Ri bealach a’ dìreadh,

Ri fraigh Choire Chruiteir,
    A' chuideachda phìceach.
Nuair a shìneas i h-eangan
'S a thèid i na deannaibh,
Cha saltradh air thalamh
    Ach barra nan ìngnean:
    Cò b' urrainn g' a leantainn
        A dh'fhearaibh na rìoghachd?
'S arraideach faramach
    Carach air grìne,
A' chòisridh nach fhanadh
    Gnè smal air an inntinn;
    Ach caochlaideach curaideach
    Caolchasach ullamh,
    An aois cha chuir truim' orra,
        Mulad no mìghean.
    'S e shlànaich an culaidh,
    Feòil mhàis agus mhuineil,
    Bhith tàmhachd am bunailt
        An cuilidh na frìthe;
    Le àilgheas a' fuireach
    Air fàsach nan grunnaibh;
    'S i 'n àsainn a' mhuime
        Tha cumail na cìche
Ris na laoigh bhreaca bhallach
        Nach meathlaich na sìanta,
Len cridheacha meara
        Le bainne na cìoba;
    Gnoiseanach eangach,
    Len girteaga geala,
    Len corpanna glana
        Le fallaineachd fìoruisg';

Le faram gun ghearan
    Feadh ghleannan na mìltich.
  Ged thigeadh an sneachda
  Chan iarradh iad aitreabh,
  'S e lag a' Choir' Altraim
    Bhios aca gan dìdean;
Feadh stacan is bhacan
    Is ghlacaga dìomhair,
Len leapaichean fasgach
    An taic Ais an t-Sìthein.

ÙRLAR

B' ionmhainn leam, ag èirigh
    San ògmhadainn
Timcheall air na slèibhtean
    'M bu chòir dhaibh bhith,
  Cupall chunntas cheud
  Luchd nan ceann gun chèill,
  Mosgladh gu neo-bheudar
    Mòr-shòlasach.
  Is osgarra om beul
  Torman socair rèidh,
  'S glan an corp 's an crè
    Seinn an dreòcaim ud.
  Broc liathchorrach èild'
  An lod ga loireadh thèid,
  Cuid ga h-arraid fhèin
    Nuair bu deònach leath'.
'S annsa leam nuair thèid
    Iad air chrònanaich,

Na na th' ann an Èirinn
	De cheòlmhoireachd:
'S binne na gach beus
Anail mhic an fhèidh
A' langanaich air eudann
	Beinn Dòbhrain;
An damh le bhùireadh fhèin
Tighinn à grunnd a chlèibh
'S fada chluinnt' a bheuc
	An àm tòiseachaidh;
An t-agh as binne geum,
'S an laogh beag na dèidh,
Freagraidh iad a chèile
	Gu deòthasach.
Plosgshùil mheallach gheur
	Gun bhonn glòinin innt',
Rosg fo mhala lèith
	Cumail seòil oirre:
Coisiche math treun
Bu bheothaile a thèid
Air thoiseach an treud
	A bha dòchasach.
Cha robh coir' ad cheum,
Cha robh moill' ad leum,
Cha robh deireadh rèis
	Air an t-seòrsa sin;
Nuair bheireadh tu steud
'S nach sealladh tu 'd dhèidh,
Cha b' aithne dhomh fhèin
	Cò bhiodh còmhla riut.
Tha 'n eilid anns an fhrìth
	Mar bu chòir dhi bhith,

Far am faigh i mìlteach
    Glan feòirneanach;
  Bruchorachd is cìob,
  Lusan am bi brìgh,
  Chuireadh sult is ìth
    Air a lòineanaibh;
  Fuaran anns am bì
  Biolaire gun dìth
  'S mìlse leath' na 'm fìon,
    'S e gun òladh i.
  Cuiseagan is riasg,
  Chinneas air an t-sliabh,
  B' annsa leath' mar bhiadh
    Na na fòlaichean.
'S ann den teachd-an-tìr
    A bha sòghar leath'
Sòbhrach 's eala-bhì
    'S barra neònagan;
  Dòbhrach bhallach mhìn
  Ghòbhlach bharrach shlìom,
  Lòintean far an cinn
    I na mòthraichean.
  Siud am pòrsan bìdh
  Mheudaicheadh an clì,
  Bheireadh iad a-nìos
    Ri àm dòilichean;
  Chuireadh air an druim
  Brata saille cruinn,
  Air an carcais luim
    Nach bu lòdail.
B' e sin an caidreabh grinn
    Mu thràth nòine,

Nuair a thionaileadh iad cruinn
     Anns a' ghlòmainn:
Air fhad 's gum biodh an oidhch',
Dad cha tigeadh ribh,
Fasgadh bhun an tuim
     B' àite còmhnaidh dhuibh.
Leapaichean nam fiadh,
Far an robh iad riamh,
An aonach farsaing fial
     'S ann am mòrmhonadh.
'S iad bu taitneach fiamh
Nuair bu daitht' am bian;
'S cha b' i 'n airc am miann
     Ach Beinn Dòbhrain.

SIUBHAL

A' bheinn luiseanach fhailleanach
     Mheallanach lìontach,
Gun choimeas dha fallaing
     Air thalamh na Crìosdachd:
'S ro-neònach tha mise,
Le bòidhchead a sliosa,
Nach eil còir aic' an ciste
     Air tiotal na rìoghachd;
'S i air dùbladh le gibhtibh,
'S air lùisreadh le miosaibh
Nach eil bitheant' a' bristeadh
     Air phriseanaibh tìre.
Làn-trusgan gun deireas,
Le usgraichean coille,

Bàrr-guc air gach doire,
    Gun choir' ort ri h-innseadh;
Far an uchdardach coileach,
Le shriutaichibh loinneil,
'S eòin bhuchallach bheag' eile
    Le 'n ceileiribh lìonmhor.
'S am buicean beag sgiolta
    Bu sgiobalt' air grìne,
Gun sgiorradh gun tubaist
    Gun tuisleadh gun dìobradh;
Crodhanach biorach,
Feadh coire ga shireadh,
Feadh fraoich agus firich,
    Air mhireadh ga dhìreadh;
Feadh rainich is barraich
    Gum b' arraideach inntinn;
Ann an ìosal gach feadain,
'S air àirde gach creagain,
Gu mireanach beiceasach
    Easgannach sìnteach.
Nuair a thèid e na bhoile
Le clisge sa choille,
'S e ruith feadh gach doire,
    Air dheireadh cha bhì e;
Leis an eangaig bu chaoile
    'S e b' aotruime sìnteag,
Mu chnocanaibh donna,
Le ruith dara-tomain,
'S e togairt an coinneamh
    Bean-chomainn os n-ìosal.
Tha mhaoisleach bheag bhrangach
    Sa ghleannan a chòmhnaidh

'S i fuireach san fhireach
    Le minneanan òga:
  Cluas bhiorach gu claisteachd,
  Sùil chorrach gu faicinn,
  'S i earbsach na casaibh
    Chur seachad na mòintich.
Ged thig Caoilte 's Cù Chulainn,
    'S gach duine den t-seòrs' ud,
Na tha dhaoine 's a dh'eachaibh
    Air fastadh Rìgh Deòrsa,
  Nan tèarnadh a craiceann
  O luaidhe 's o lasair
  Cha chual' is chan fhac' i
    Na ghlacadh r' a beò i;
'S i gradcharach fadchasach
    Aigeannach neònach
  Gealchèireach gasganach,
  Gealtach ro mhadadh,
  Air chaisead na leacainn
    Cha saltradh i còmhnard;
'S i noigeanach gnoigeasach
    Gogcheannach sòrnach,
  Biorshùileach sgurshùileach
  Frionasach furachair,
  A' fuireach sa mhunadh
    An do thuinich a seòrsa.

ÙRLAR

B' i sin a' mhaoisleach luaineach
    Feadh òganan
Bileachan nam bruach
    'S àite còmhnaidh dhi;
    Duilleagan nan craobh,
    Bileagan an fhraoich,
    Criomagan a gaoil,
      Cha b' e 'm fòtras.
    A h-aigneadh aotrom suairc
    Aobhach ait, gun ghruaim,
    Ceann bu bhraise ghuanaiche
      Ghòraiche;
    A' chrè bu cheanalt' stuaim,
    Chalaich i gu buan
    An gleann a' bharraich uain'
      Bu nòsaire.
'S tric a ghabh i cluain
    Sa Chreig Mhòir
On as miosail leath' bhith Luan
    Is a Dhòmhnach ann;
    Pris an dèan i suain
    Bitheanta mun cuairt,
    Bhristeas a' ghaoth tuath,
      'S nach leig deò oirre;
    Am fasgadh Doire Chrò,
    An taice ris an t-Sròin,
    Am measg nam faillean òg'
      Is nan còsagan.
    Masgadh 'n Fhuarain Mhòir,
    'S e pailte gu leòr,

’S blasta leath’ na bheòir,
    Gu bhith pòit oirre.
Deoch den t-sruthan uasal
    R’ a òl aice;
Dh’fhàgas fallain fuasgailteach
    Ògail i;
Gradcharach ri uair,
’S ealamh bheir i cuairt
Nuair thachradh i an ruaig
    ’S a bhiodh tòir oirre.
’S maothbhuidh’ daitht’ a snuadh,
Dearg a dreach ’s a tuar,
’S gura h-iomadh buaidh
    Tha mar chòmhla oirr’;
Fulangach air fuachd,
’S i gun chum’ air luaths,
Urram claisteachd cluas
    Na Roinn Eòrpa dhi.

SIUBHAL

Bu ghrinn leam am pannal
    A’ tarraing an òrdugh,
A’ dìreadh le faram
    Ri carraig na Sròine:
Eadar sliabh Craobh na h-Ainnis
Is beul Choire Dhaingein,
Bu bhiadhchar greigh cheannard
    Nach ceannaich am pòrsan;
Dà thaobh Choire Rainich,
Mu sgèith sin a’ Bhealaich,

Coire Rèidh Beinn Ach' Chaladair,
   'S thairis mun Chonnlon
Air Lurgainn na Laoidhre
    Bu ghreadhnach a' chòisridh;
  Mu Làrach na Fèinne,
  Sa Chraig Sheilich na dhèidh sin,
  Far an cruinnich na h-èildean
    Bu neo-spèiseil mun fhòlach.
  'S gum b' e 'n aighear 's an èibhneas
  Bhith faicheachd air rèidhlean
  A' co-mhacnas ri chèile
    'S a' leumnaich feadh mòintich;
  Ann am pollachaibh daimseir,
  Le sodradh gu meamnach,
  Gu togarrach mearcasach
    Aintheasach gòrach.
  Cha bhiodh ìot' air an teangaidh
  Taobh shìos a' Mhill Teanail,
  Le fìon Uillt na h-Annaid,
    Blas meala r' a òl air:
  Sruth brìoghmhor geal tana,
  'S e sìoladh tron ghaineimh
  'S e 's mìlse na 'n caineal,
    Cha b' aineolach òirnn e.
  Siud an ìocshlainte mhaireann
  Thig à ìochdar an talaimh
  Gheibhte lìonmhorachd mhaith dhith
    Gun a ceannach le stòras,
  Air fàrainn na beinne
  As dàicheile sealladh
  A dh'fhàs anns a' cheithreamh
    A bheil mi 'n Roinn Eòrpa:

Le glainead a h-uisge,
Gu maothbhlasta brisggheal,
Caoin caomhail glan miosail,
    Neo-mhisgeach ri pòit air:
Le fuaranaibh grinne
Am bun gruamach na biolair,
Còinneach uaine mun imeall
    As iomadach seòrsa.
Bu ghlan uachdar na linne,
Gu neo-bhuaireasach milis,
Tighinn na chuairteig on ghrinneal
    Air slinnean Beinn Dòbhrain.
Tha lethtaobh na Leacainn
    Le mais' air a còmhdach,
'S am Frith-Choirean creagach
    Na sheasamh ga chòir sin:
Gu stobanach stacanach
Slocanach laganach
Cnocanach cnapanach
    Caiteanach ròmach,
Pasganach badanach
    Bachlagach bòidheach;
A h-aisridhean corrach
Nam fasraichibh molach,
'S i b' fhasa dhomh mholadh,
    Bha sonas gu leòr oirr';
Cluigeanach gucagach
    Uchdanach còmhnard;
Le dìthean glan ruiteach,
Breac mìsleanach sultmhor,
Tha 'n fhrìth air a busgadh
    San trusgan bu chòir dhi.

ÙRLAR

Am monadh farsaing faoin
    Glacach srònagach
Lag a' Choire Fhraoich
    Cuid bu bhòidhche dheth.
Sin am fearann caoin
Air an d' fhàs an aoibh
Far am bi na laoigh
    'S na daimh chròcach;
'S e deisearach ri grèin',
Seasgaireachd dha rèir,
'S neo-bheag air an èildeig
    Bhith chòmhnaidh ann;
Leannan an fhir lèith
As faramaiche ceum,
Nach iarradh a' chlèir
    A thoirt pòsaidh dhaibh;
'S glan fallain a crè,
Is banail i na beus,
Cha robh h-anail breun
    Ge b' è phògadh i.
'S e 'n coire choisinn gaol
    A h-uil' òganaich,
A chunna' riamh a thaobh
    'S a ghlac eòlas air:
'S lìonmhor feadan caol
Air an èirich gaoth,
Far am bi na laoich
    Cumail còmhdhalach;
Bruthaichean nan learg
Far am biodh greigh dhearg,

Ceann-uidhe gach sealg
Fad am beòshlainte;
’S e làn den h-uile maoin
A thig a-mach le braon,
Fàileadh nan sùbh-chraobh
Is nan ròsan ann.
Gheibhte tacar èisg
Air a còrsa,
’S bhith gan ruith le leus
Anns na mòrshruthan:
Morgha cumhann geur,
Le chrann giuthais fhèin,
Aig fir shubhach threubhach
Nan dòrnaibh;
Bu shòlasach a’ leum
Bric air buinne rèidh,
A’ ceapadh chuileag eutrom
Nan dòrlaichean.
Chan eil muir no tìr
A bheil tuilleadh brìgh
’S a tha feadh do chrìch
Air a h-òrdachadh.

AN CRÙNLUDH

Tha ’n eilid anns a’ ghleannan seo
’S chan amadan gun eòlas
A leanadh i mur b’ aithne dha
Tighinn farasta na còmhdhail:
Gu faiteach bhith na h-earalas,
Tighinn am faisge dhi mun caraich i,

Gu faicilleach, glè earraigeach,
    Mum fairich i ga còir e:
Feadh shloc is ghlac is chamhanan,
Is chlach a dhèanadh falach air,
Bhith beachdail air an talamh
    'S air a' char a thig na neòil air;
'S an t-astar bhith ga tharraing air
Cho macanta 's a b' aithne dha,
Gun glacadh e dha h-aindeoin i
    Le h-anabharra seòltachd;
Le tùr, gun ghainne baralach,
An t-sùil a chur gu danarra,
A' stiùradh na dubh-bannaiche,
    'S a h-aire ri fear cròice.
Bhiodh rùdan air an tarraing
Leis an lùbt' an t-iarann-earra,
Bheireadh ionnsaigh nach biodh mearachdach
    Don fhear a bhiodh ga seòladh;
Spor ùr an dèis a teannachadh,
Buill' ùird a' sgailceadh daingean ris,
Cha diùlt an t-srad nuair bheanas i
    Don deannaig a bha neònach.
'S e 'm fùdar tioram teannabaich
Air chùl an asgairt ghreannanaich,
Chuireadh smùid ri acainn mheallanaich
    À baraille Nic Còiseim.
'S i 'n teachdaire bha dealasach,
    Nach mealladh e na dhòchas,
Nuair lasadh e mar dhealanach
    Gu feareigin a leònadh;
    Gu silteach leis na peileirean
Bhiodh luchd nan luirgnean speireacha,

'S nam bus bu tirme bheileanaich,
    Gun mheiliche, gun tòicean.
'S e camp na Craige Seiliche
Bha ceannsalach nan ceithreamhnaibh;
Le aingealtas cha teirinn iad
    Gu eirthir às an eòlas,
Mur ceannsaichear iad deireasach
Ri àm an crìche deireannaich,
An tabhannaich le deifir
    A bhith deileann air an tòrach;
Gun channtaireachd, gun cheilearachd,
Ach dranndail chon a' deileis rith',
A ceann a chur gu peirealais,
    Aig eilid Beinne Dòbhrain.
'S O! b' ionmhainn le fir cheanalta
    Nach b' aineolach mu spòrsa,
Bhith timcheall air na bealaichibh
    Le fearalachd na h-òige;
Far am bi na fèidh gu faramach,
'S na fir nan dèidh gu caithriseach,
Le gunna bu mhath barantas
    Thoirt aingil nuair bu chòir dhi;
Le cuilean foirmeil togarrach,
'G am biodh a stiùir air bhogadan,
'S e miolairtich gu sodanach,
    'S nach ob e dol nan còmhdhail.
Na fhuirbidh làidir cosgarrach,
Ro-inntinneach neo-fhoisinneach,
Gu guineach sgiamhach gobeasgaidh
    San obair bh' aig a sheòrsa;
'S a fhrioghan cuilg a' togail air,
Gu mailgheach gruamach doicheallach,

'S a gheanachan cnuasaicht' fosgailte
    Co-bhogartaich r' an sgòrnan.
Gum b' arraideach a' charachd ud
    'S bu chabhagach i 'n còmhnaidh,
Nuair shìneadh iad na h-eanganan
    Le h-athghoirid na mòintich;
Na beanntaichean 's na bealaichean,
    Gum freagradh iad mac-talla dhuit,
Le fuaim na gairme galanaich
    Aig faram a' choin ròmaich,
Gan tèarnadh às na mullaichibh
    Gu linnichean nach grunnaich iad,
'S ann bhios iad feadh na tuinne
    Anns an luinneinich 's iad leòinte;
'S na cuileanan gu fulasgach
    Gan cumail air na muinealaibh,
'S nach urrainn iad dol tuilleadh às,
    Ach fuireach 's bhith gun deò annt'.
Is ged a thuirt mi beagan riu,
    Mun innsinn uil' an dleastnas orr',
Chuireadh iad am bhreislich mi
    Le deisimireachd chòmhraidh.

NOTES

— *Abbreviations* —

FFD: Frank Fraser Darling, *A Herd of Red Deer* (Edinburgh: Luath Press, 2016 [1937]).

RD: T.F. Clutton-Brock, F.E. Guinness and S.D. Albon, *Red Deer: Behaviour and Ecology of Two Sexes* (Chicago: The University of Chicago Press, 1982).

SNH: Scottish Natural Heritage Policy Paper, *Red Deer and the Natural Heritage* (Perth: Scottish Natural Heritage, 1994).

— *Part 1* —

Page 22 – "I saw a deer drive once": drives of up to 300 deer took place in the medieval period and continued until the end of the eighteenth century. *SNH*, 16.

— *Part 2* —

Page 23 – "Graham": quote adapted from Aida Edemariam, "I am living in the late season, but it has its songs, too", Interview with Jorie Graham, *Guardian*, Friday 1 December 2017.

Page 24 – "Those who nourish": quote adapted from Charles Darwin, *The Descent of Man*, Part II, Chapter VIII.

Page 25 – "Luther Adams": quote adapted from John Luther Adams, *Winter Music: Composing the North* (Middletown, CT: Wesleyan University Press, 2004), 140.

Page 25 – "Clutton-Brock": quote adapted from *RD*, 31.

Page 26 – "*king-o'-the-castle and tig-round-a-hillock*": *FFD*, 84.

Page 27 – "hair grass … cushion moss": based on the list in *FFD*, 143-7.

Page 28 – "Àis an t-Sìthein": I've been unable to verify that Macintyre lived at this steading, which is still marked on maps and now used as an enclosure for sheep, but the claim is repeated in various walking guides, including Cameron McNeish, *The Munros: Scotland's Highest Mountains* (Edinburgh: Lomond Books, 2002), 46.

— *Part 3* —

Page 29 – "a sharp staccato": these lines are based on behaviour recorded in *FFD*, 80-1.

Page 33 – "there are deer paths": the ancientness of deer paths is speculated upon in *FFD*, 58.

Page 33 – "Ice Age pioneers": Scotland's deer population dates at least from the end of the last Ice Age, about 11,000 years ago, when a land bridge existed between Great Britain and continental Europe.

Page 33 – "piss and oestrus … rut': adapted from Gary Snyder, *The Practice of the Wild* (Berkeley, CA: Counterpoint, 2010), 120, "a literature of bloodstains, a bit of piss, a whiff of estrus, a hit of rut, a scrape on a sapling, and long gone".

Page 33 – "whose testes have swelled": G.A. Lincoln, "The seasonal reproductive changes in the red deer stag (Cervus elaphus)", *Journal of Zoology*, Vol. 163 (January 1971), 105-123.

Page 33 – "he runs an antler … ejaculates": these lines are based on behaviour recorded in *FFD*, 157.

Page 34 – "Their paths lead to rubbing trees … sweetest": information on deer paths, wallows and rubbing trees can be found in *FFD*, 58-63.

Page 34 – "When a deer lacks … these places": adapted from *FFD*, 189, 190, 2, 124.

Page 34 — "underlying life": Tennyson, *In Memoriam A.H.H.*:

> Old Yew, which graspest at the stones
>> That name the under-lying dead,
>> Thy fibres net the dreamless head,
> Thy roots are wrapt about the bones.

— *Part 4* —

Page 37 — "register of time": Henri Bergson, *Creative Evolution*, translated by Arthur Mitchell (London: Macmillan, 1911), 17: "there is, open somewhere, a register in which time is being inscribed".

Page 37 — "the sunlight through the willow leaves": my adaptation of a marginal note by an unknown Irish scribe, 9th century, included in Kenneth Hurlstone Jackson, *A Celtic Miscellany* (London: Penguin, 1976), 177.

Page 41 — "all day she grunts and grumbles": see *FFD*, 82.

— *Part 5* —

Page 48 — "think themselves within me": Maurice Merleau-Ponty, *Phenomenology of Perception*, translated by Colin Smith (London: Routledge & Keegan Paul, 1962), 214: "As I contemplate the blue of the sky ... I abandon myself to it and plunge into this mystery, it 'thinks itself within me,' I am the sky itself as it is drawn together and unified, and as it begins to exist for itself; my consciousness is saturated with this limitless blue".

Page 49 – "they serve it": Alastair McIntosh, *Soil and Soul: People Versus Corporate Power* (London: Aurum Press, 2004), 234 n. 4.2: "Man is the *servant* of the ground".

Page 50 – "autumn tides of grass": *RD*, 61.

Page 50 – "a matriarchal tribe": *FFD*, 78.

Page 50 – "he lowers ... races off": *RD*, 54.

Page 50 – "he rakes ... presence": *RD*, 107, 110.

Page 51 – "noses ... readiness": for these and other details in this section I am indebted to deer farmer, author and vet John Fletcher, whose correspondence is rich with knowledge, experience and enthusiasm.

Page 51 – "He licks ... mount him": *FFD*, 173.

Page 52 – "infinity": Timothy Morton, *Being Ecological* (London: Pelican, 2018), 91: "ecologically-aware criticism opens up a vertigo-inducing abyss of potentially infinite, overlapping contexts".

Page 52 – "the queerness of pregnancy": Maggie Nelson, *The Argonauts* (London: Melville House, 2016), 16: "Is there something inherently queer about pregnancy itself, insofar as it profoundly alters one's 'normal' state, and occasions a radical intimacy with – and radical alienation from – one's body?"

Page 53 – "Sometimes Duncan ... growth": these lines are after the first poem in Niall O'Gallagher's Gaelic sequence "Dealbhan Ghlascu" ["Pictures of Glasgow"] in *Beatha Ùr* (Inbhir Nis: Clàr, 2013), 29.

Page 55 – "chorus of bells": Novalis, *Werke und Briefe*, trans. Kristofor Minta and Herbert Pföstl: "A small spring came out of a hillside and it sounded like so many bells."

Part 8

Page 61 — "Amergin": The indented 'I am' lines in this section are inspired by 'The Song of Amergin', traditionally held to be the oldest lines of poetry in Gaelic. The poem can be found in Douglas Hyde, *The Story of Early Gaelic Literature* (London: T. Fisher Unwin, 1895), 26:

> I am the wind which breathes upon the sea,
> I am the wave of the ocean,
> I am the murmur of the billows,
> I am the ox of the seven combats,
> I am the vulture upon the rock,
> I am a beam of the sun,
> I am the fairest of plants,
> I am a wild boar in valour,
> I am a salmon in the water,
> I am a lake in the plain,
> I am a word of science,
> I am the point of the lance of battle,
> I am the God who creates in the head [i.e., of man] the fire [i.e., the thought].
> Who is it who throws light into the meeting on the mountain?
> Who announces the ages of the moon [If not I]?
> Who teaches the place where couches the sun [If not I]?

Hyde describes the song as "noticeable for its curious pantheistic strain which reminds one strangely of the East". Robert Graves offers a more extended, mystical interpretation of it in *The White Goddess* (London: Faber and Faber, 1948).

Page 61 — "lace-workers": the lace-makers of Burano describe the product of their craft as punto in aria, stitching in the air. Tim Ingold, *Lines* (London: Routledge, 2016), 54.

Page 62 — "hyperobjectivity": Timothy Morton, *Hyperobjects: Philosophy and Ecology After the End of the World* (Minneapolis: University of Minnesota Press, 2013).

Page 62 – "work your way": the imagery relating to stalking in this section is indebted to Charles Foster, *Being a Beast: An Intimate and Radical Look at Nature* (London: Profile, 2016), 145-77.

Page 63 – "Heraclitus": my paraphrase of Heraclitus, fragment 59 in John Burnet, *Early Greek Philosophy* (London: A. & C. Black, 1920), 137.

— General Sources —

John Fletcher, *Deer* (London: Reaktion, 2014).

James Hunter, *On the Other Side of Sorrow* (Edinburgh: Birlinn, 2014).

Tim Ingold, *Being Alive* (London: Routledge, 2011), and *Lines* (London: Routledge, 2016).

Seumas MacNeill and Frank Richardson, *Piobaireachd and its Interpretations: Classical Music of the Highland Bagpipe* (Edinburgh: John Donald, 1987).

Derick S. Thomson, 'Macintyre, Duncan Bàn [Donnchadh Bàn Mac an t-Saoir] (1723?–1812)', *Oxford Dictionary of National Biography*, 2006.

ACKNOWLEDGEMENTS

My thanks to the editors of *The Clearing, Glasgow Review of Books, Outlandia Blog, Reliquiae* and the anthology *Antlers of Water*, where sections of this poem have previously been published. Sections of the poem and foreword have also appeared, in slightly different forms, in my article "Ben Dorain: an Ecopoetic Translation" in the journal *Humanities*.

I am grateful to the Oppenheim-John Downes Memorial Trust for financial assistance in researching the poem, and to London Fieldworks and the Nevis Landscape Partnership for an Outlandia Residency, where some of the poem was written. I also benefited from a Scottish Emerging Writer Residency at Cove Park.

Thanks to those who have offered advice about Gaelic poetry, red deer, and the geology of the West Highlands, including Robert Crawford, John Fletcher, Peter MacKay and Morag Ross.

Finally, thanks to Vicky, for everything.

ORTHOGRAPHY

The Gaelic text and stanzaic layout of *Moladh Beinn Dòbhrain* follow Angus Macleod's edition in his *Òrain Dhonnchaidh Bhàin / The Songs of Duncan Bàn MacIntyre* (Scottish Gaelic Texts Society) of 1978. The spelling has been standardised to comply with the Gaelic Orthographic Conventions. Non-standard spellings have occasionally been retained, however, to reflect the rhyme scheme and the stress patterns of MacIntyre's neologisms.

ABOUT DUNCAN BÀN MACINTYRE

Duncan Bàn MacIntyre was born in Argyll, probably in 1723. Between 1746 and 1766 he worked as a forester and gamekeeper in the West Highlands, and his intimacy with this landscape is at the heart of his poetry. Illiterate, he committed thousands of lines of verse to memory, and was known by the nickname Donnchadh Bàn nan Oran (Fair-haired Duncan of the Songs). In 1767 MacIntyre moved with his family to Edinburgh, where he enrolled in the city guard. Although he continued to compose songs and poems, his greatest work comes from the period before 1767, when he produced many poems in praise of Highland landscapes and their wildlife. His work also meditates upon the threat which large-scale sheep farming brought to the way of life in the Highlands. After 1767 he spent the rest of his life in Edinburgh. He died in 1812 and is buried in Greyfriars Kirkyard.

MacIntyre's long poem *Moladh Beinn Dòbhrain (Praise of Ben Dorain)* is often described as one of the masterpieces of Scots Gaelic literature. Full of light, movement, and biodiversity, it demonstrates an unsentimental environmental awareness grounded in close observation of a mountain and its herd of red deer. Sorley MacLean, arguably the most significant Gaelic poet since MacIntyre, believed *Moladh Beinn Dòbhrain* to be "the greatest example of naturalistic realism in the poetry of Europe", a non-Romantic poem which achieves a "realisation of dynamic nature".

Musical adaptations of the poem include Ronald Stevenson's choral symphony *Ben Dorain*, first performed by the BBC Scottish Symphony Orchestra in 2007; other settings are regularly sung at Gaelic music festivals. Previous translations – including those by Hugh MacDiarmid, Iain Crichton Smith and Alan Riach – have emphasised the formal unity of MacIntyre's poem. Garry MacKenzie's free translation explores how a completely new form might allow *Moladh Beinn Dòbhrain* to be read in a modern poetic context, while also creating a dialogue between MacIntyre's work and twenty-first-century environmental concerns.